Purpose
Potential
Prosperity

Create your own economy in the new economy

Crystal McRae

ISBN: 9798497033069
Unblock Academy
Box 347
Vibank SK
S0G 4Y0
306-209-9287

Cover Design: Crystal McRae

THIS BOOK IS DEDICATED TO YOU

You attracted this book into your life because you know that you can become more, do more and have more. For that, we congratulate you! Thank you for reading.

TABLE OF CONTENTS

FOREWORD

How comfortable are you with money?

For the first 26 years of my life, I wasn't comfortable with it at all.

The problem with being uncomfortable with money is that instead of attracting it, you push money away. As a result, I owed more money than I earned.

However, when I started to get comfortable with the idea of money, everything began to change. Before long, I knew I'd never worry about money again.

So how about you?

Can you see yourself being in a position of never having to worry about money again?

Instead of brushing this question off, think about it for a few moments and answer it honestly. Your response will help you begin to understand.

Whether or not you currently feel comfortable with money, what you're about to learn can put you on the road to financial freedom.

Bob Proctor
CEO of the Proctor Gallagher Institute
New York Times Best Selling Author, *'You Were Born Rich'*

INTRODUCTION

If you are ready to break free and break through, become more, do more, and have more; I am thrilled that you decided to pick up this book.

Permit me to briefly introduce myself and my experience with the material and information Bob Proctor and I share. My name is Crystal McRae and I live an incredibly blessed life. I am a mom of two amazing boys. I spend my days doing what I love and am grateful every day for our time freedom. We do what we want, when we want and are always planning our next experience or moving towards our next big goal.

Now, life wasn't always like this for me. I lived like most people and the struggle was real. I worked hard, uncertain of how things would turn out and all I knew was just to keep going and do more. My income as an entrepreneur was always up and down but never consistent. I was forever on this mission to figure out how to achieve the level of success and lifestyle I wanted. I was caught in a trap of my own making and I didn't even know it. Most, if not all of us are.

Four years ago, I was introduced to the teachings of Bob Proctor on a personal level. He became my mentor and coach as I pursued my certification in the field of mindset, success and human potential.

He helped me realize that it wasn't about learning about mindset, it was turning that knowledge into real results that stick. And did they ever stick! My income grew substantially and I wasn't even trying that hard. I was working less and having more fun! I became confident in ways I had never experienced before - true real self-confidence from the inside out. I started to experience genuine happiness, wealth, and health mentally, emotionally and physically. And it just keeps getting better.

The stories in this book are from ordinary people who, like myself and Bob Proctor, have experienced and continue to experience extraordinary results.

We have discovered our purpose, untapped our infinite potential and prosper in ways we couldn't have imagined in the past.

I encourage you to relax and begin this journey of purpose, potential and prosperity through each of these incredible stories.

You too, can live the life you love!

Crystal McRae
Founder and CEO of Unblock Academy

CHAPTER 1
"How I Rediscovered Me"
By Melanie Morrison

"Your journey begins with a choice to get up, step out and live fully."

- Oprah Winfrey

Finding my purpose did not happen overnight.

In fact, it came to me in my fifties. At the age of forty-seven, I found myself running a daycare out of my home. While I love children, I just did not expect to be still watching children in my home as an empty-nester. Let me give you a brief history.

I married a military man. You may ask, so what is wrong with that? After all, travel, job security, pension, medical benefits-all good things. While he had the career for twenty-seven years, I had many jobs during that time. Those jobs were not only pleasant, but they lead me to the path I am on now, along with many experiences. Some of the jobs were dietary aide and cleaner in hospitals, retail, daycare (in and out of the home), engineer clerk, construction site admin assistant, box store department manager and teacher assistant, to name a few. When we moved, I did whatever job I could find. I was willing to work at anything to help support my family.

Support. Let's talk about that. For me, it is a loaded word. I spent twenty-seven years supporting my husband and encouraging him to do what he wanted to do - seven tours around the world, away from his family six to eight months at a time. I never once said don't go. After all, the money was good but it did mean that the kids were without a father and left with a cranky mother. Something that always helped me cope with it was the fact that single moms were doing it on their own for longer than six to eight months, so I needed to stop whining about it. Supporting him was the best thing I would always continue to do. I wasn't always cranky.

However, working and caring for the house, kids and extra activities or driving them here and there was tiring and sometimes hard. When the kids went to bed, I went to bed. As they got older, I sometimes went to bed before them.

Not only supporting my husband, as most moms do, I always supported my kids in whatever they wanted to do. University, college, schools, jobs, you name it, I supported it. I was there and available to serve, support and help my family. I was the strong one, never cried when my husband would go away for months or when it came time to move (making new friends was hard for the kids), and setting up the house to try to get back to normal as soon as possible. After all, that is what a wife and mother should do, right? Can you relate?

The one question and the most important one for me was: Who would support my dreams? Who would help me?

Some replies from my family were:

"You cannot do that, you are too old."

"Why would you want to do that?"

The thoughts and self-sabotage we create in our heads are real. I started to believe the words they would say, "Hmmm, maybe they are right, it is a crazy idea. What was I thinking?"

Then it would turn around, "Oh, you have to go away again?"

"Oh, you need this, ok, I can help."

"Yeah, a lot is going on right now. I am better off not starting something new."

So as time got away from me, I kept on keeping on until my kids moved away from home. This was the time my husband was to move again. The kids told us they were not going to move with us. We were in shock. We did move to the other side of the country and we were leaving the kids behind.

Fast forward six months after we moved, my kids decided to move out to Alberta with us. My house was full again, two young adult girls and their boyfriends. Since I did not want to go out and work in the workforce (I thought I was too old), I ran a daycare in my home again. It was a need in my area and I could have the flexibility if I needed time off. Besides, I did enjoy it, however I was getting older and tired.

After the kids settled in Alberta with jobs in the area, they decided it was time for them to move out again. It was my husband and the daycare kids again in the home. About one year after this, I found myself wanting more and it was MY time. I found out my youngest daughter was due to have my first grandchild and I needed a change. What would I do? That was when a Network Marketing company showed up on my Facebook feed from a lady I know.

There was something about this company that drew me in. I did direct sales when my kids were first born but I didn't do it right. After twenty-five years of not showing interest in the industry, I thought I should give this a try. After all, it has been twenty-five years and I am older now, so why not? This was something that I wanted to do for myself. I had no idea at the time that this would lead me to my purpose.

When I partnered with my company, I did it for the community connection and products. As a new haircare company, there were only nine products at the time. My hair was over-processed and thinning. I just needed something for better hair, community connections and overall, just something for me. It was my time now! I needed this!

As of now, I have been with the company for six years. My hair is healthier, I am happier and I feel like I have myself back. I can spend time with my grandkids daily, I have time and freedom and I got to tell you my story. Well, at least part of it.

My purpose has become my Gratitude. I continue to help and support others on a different level; a level that requires trust, commitment and gratitude. Let's be honest, I did not join the company with Gratitude in mind. It found me.

This is who I became. Gratitude. The company was just a gateway to figure this out. I started with the company at age forty-seven and at age fifty-one, I began to find Gratitude. Now at fifty-three, I am doing me and living life on purpose (gratitude), still helping and supporting others in a higher and more responsible way.

Finding my purpose did not come overnight, as I mentioned. The more I started to put myself "out there" by making connections, the more Gratitude opportunities began to happen for me. I began to find new ways I could help people. I started to volunteer more, I always enjoyed volunteering. I started planning more events to help with my Gratitude goals and it became like a flowing river of ideas. Through all of this and taking charge of me, I found that my passion was to help others and that is when I realised that my purpose was Gratitude.

One Gratitude event I recently did was at a women's shelter. I got some ladies and a stylist together and we organized a haircut event. It was gratifying just seeing the smiles of the residents and staff. Most of these ladies arrive without anything and have to start over. So helping them feel good about themselves is truly something I am grateful to help with. I grew into my potential, I am still growing and it becomes larger and clearer every day. I take opportunities when they are presented to me, opportunities come for a reason. I don't like the circumstance of "what if I do or what if I don't."

I like to make my own circumstances. This is something I have learned through the Unblock Academy. I look for more opportunities and that is where my full potential lies. There is more out there and more to profit from, you just need to tune into yourself. Opportunities helped me grow and they will do the same for you.

I would like to invite you to take charge of yourself. You have so much potential. Just look for the opportunity that could help you and you will attract your purpose. Your purpose will be more evident as you go.

Meet Melanie Morrison

Melanie Morrison is a mother of two girls, grandmother of two girls and a Military Veteran's wife. While moving every three to five years, she always found herself starting over while continuing to be the "rock" for the family. One thing she instilled into her girls was to always be kind, look out for yourself and never step on anyone's toes, because you never know when you will need their help.

As an empty-nester, she found herself wanting more. After joining a network marketing company, she found her true passion, Gratitude and self-development, which she has learned to share with her teammates and everyone around her. Her passion has set her on a leadership journey of discovery of fulfillment and prosperity. Melanie is an inspiration to all Military spouses, who not only support their partners but can be successful confident women.

"Your Time is Now."

PURPOSE POTENTIAL PROSPERITY

CHAPTER 2
"Phoenix Transformation"
By Jennean Bruner

"Life does not have to be a struggle. This was one of the most important lessons I ever learned. It can be easy."
- Jennean Bruner

There was a time in my life where I was so lost, I didn't even know there was a direction or purpose for my life.

As a first-generation residential school survivor, I spent many years dealing with the effects upon my family's life. After surviving immense trauma, I also spent many years of my life lost and confused.

At nineteen, I experienced losing one of the most influential and important female role models in my life, my grandmother. I was drinking more than I care to admit, staying up all night and sleeping during the day and wishing I were no longer alive.

I finally decided I was good at something in life and started down the path to becoming a professional chef. I adopted the prestige of "Chef" with passion and began working anywhere from eleven to sixteen hours a day, five or six days a week. Little did I know I was choosing an all too familiar path of abuse and self-abuse.

I worked hard - so much so that it became my identity. I spent twelve years missing out on all major holidays and connections with those I love around me. I had utterly lost myself and any meaning my life needed to have.

I wrote a journal entry to myself during this time, saying that I had gone almost two weeks without speaking to another human being and that if I had died, no one would even know. This was how low I had gotten and how emotionally lost I was.

Around this time, I started feeling like there had to be more to life than my current existence of loneliness and suffering. Something inside me told me I needed to change drastically. So, I picked up my life and moved three hundred kilometers away, where I did not know a single soul.

I decided I'd had enough of the dysfunction of the restaurant industry. I was ready to make the shift into living a better existence, even if it meant making less money. Before this transition to a new city, I lost my job and all the money I saved quickly started draining away. I packed all my belongings in one day, moved to Vancouver, British Columbia and made up the money needed to afford to move all my things to Kelowna, British Columbia.

When I first arrived in Kelowna, I took my last thirty-five dollars and bought a flat of 30 eggs, a case of ramen noodles and this was what I ate for a month. I was moving during a time of year when no one was hiring chefs and I could not find any other work. I ate one single boiled egg in the morning and one pack of ramen at night for dinner. This experience sums up my life well. Surviving is the word that comes to mind. I was not living, I was only just existing and surviving.

Shortly after I had moved to Kelowna, my Mother ended her long battle with mental health and drug problems. This traumatic event created a massive emotional shift inside of me. The pain I was feeling inside was the deciding factor in my decision to seek more in life. I began meditating with an intense desire to connect and communicate with my mother seeking answers.

This led me to my soul's purpose. From that moment on, my life has been a series of synchronicities that has led me to step into my purpose in life today. These synchronicities led me to an event called "How to Make Your First Million Dollars."

Leading up to this, I felt frustrated with life and ready to let go of anything to change because I knew there was more to life than how I was living it. I knew I had so much to offer the world that was not being utilized because I was getting in my own way. I knew that I had been trying for years to change my circumstances from struggling to thriving and was failing and that it was time to look outside of myself.

I followed the directions from this powerful week-long event exactly. Now at this time, I was living paycheck to paycheck. I had so much debt, I could not even talk about it because it overwhelmed me. I had been working so hard, I threw myself so far into adrenal fatigue that I needed a prescription to fix it. I sometimes would go days with no food because things were so tight.

Let me tell you, I listened and made a powerful decision to say yes even though I could not see the "how." I could not even comprehend how I would get the thousands of dollars for this course but intuitively knew I had to try. I took the leap in utter faith that there would be a way if this were meant to be. In just under two and a half hours, I manifested the total price for this course and I went on to the most important thing I ever did to change my life.

It only took me three weeks to make the same amount I would in a year as a professional chef, which also would have involved struggling and losing myself along the way. Life does not have to be a struggle. This was one of the most important lessons I ever learned. It can be easy. All you need to do is decide to stop doing the same thing you always do. Invest in your personal growth and you can change your life too.

I am no different than anyone else. This process works for anyone willing to listen, apply themselves and be open-minded enough to embrace a new awareness.

Meet Jennean Bruner

Jennean is a certified Usui Shiki Rhoyo Reiki Master/Teacher & Karuna Ki Reiki Master/Teacher. As a spiritual mentor and teacher offering a spiritual formula for lasting manifestation and quantum leaps, she uses her knowledge of astrology and chakras to energetically align others to quickly heal and align them to their purpose.

Her spiritual mentorship program, personalized reiki courses and a line of handmade Reiki-infused candles (with all-natural soy and essential oils) that offer specialized Reiki-infused intentions.

Her calling is to help people come into their divine life purpose and become more connected to their truth and the reason they are here. She helps people heal through their traumas and pain that is blocking them from their true potential.

CHAPTER 3
"Enough is Enough"
By Crystal McRae

"You are here on purpose with a purpose. You have infinite potential. You can become, do, and have anything you really want."

- Crystal McRae

Have you ever had an "enough is enough" moment?

A time where you were so fed up and frustrated with the feeling of being defeated and tired? The conversation in your head went something like, "That's it! No more. I am not living like this anymore! Enough is enough."

Then, there was one time different from all the other times you were in this place. This time something actually changed. This time *you* changed. You may not be able to know precisely why or how it happened, you just know it was different than all the other times.

I remember being confused because I thought that my "why" was strong enough. I thought that wanting more for my kids was enough. I thought it was a strong enough "why" that made me cry but I discovered that it was not enough. Everyone wants better for their kids, for their family, for themselves. Everyone wants to worry less about money and have more time to spend with their loved ones. To take the trips, do the renovations, pay off the credit cards and live in a nice home. That was not enough to get me to my "enough is enough" moment.

I thought I was on the right track but I wasn't on purpose. When we don't have our purpose right, everything else is off.

Then, one day it happened- The "enough is enough" moment that changed everything. We can't always connect the dots moving forward but we can always connect the dots looking backward. So here's my story looking backward on how I created the life that I love, living a life of time and money freedom, living on purpose and realizing my true potential.

If you're anything like me, you're on the hunt for answers - for real help. You're looking for the path of least resistance. You're looking for the way out just like I was.

One day on my continual search to this mystery of success, I happened upon a social media advertisement that spoke to me. I still can't exactly remember what it said. All I know is that it hit me in the gut and I was smart enough to click the button that said "Contact Me." That inner knowing opened my life and my future to my purpose, my potential and profit in so many ways.

"Crystal, what do you want? What do you really want?"

I think that was the first time that I was ever asked that question. Something came over me on that phone call and I spoke with such conviction to this then stranger on the other end.

"I want to help people! I want to make a difference! I want to leave a legacy. An impact! I just really want to help other people succeed!" I was almost yelling this through the phone. I surrendered, I spoke it into existence. I was done living small, I was done struggling to figure it out. I was done wasting time, energy and money. No more. Enough was enough.
I knew there had to be a better way. I knew that it wasn't just about trying harder, doing more and sacrificing. I didn't want

to live the short-term pain for a long-term game anymore. I was tired of trying harder and I didn't want to face burnout again. I was frustrated. Enough was enough.

I was a single stay-at-home Mom. I was a full-time entrepreneur and I had bills to pay like everybody else. There was zero evidence that I would achieve my big goals and live a life of time and money freedom because I had tried and failed so many times before. I had been trying for years to break through and break free. I knew that if I didn't change things that day, nothing would change.

Looking back, I didn't know who I was for the majority of my life. I was what I thought other people thought that I was good at. I was what my friends thought I should be. I was what I thought my parents wanted me to be. I was what I thought my community thought I should be. I wore many hats but I didn't even know who I was.

Discovering your purpose is finding who you really are, why you're really here, and what you really want. Discovering your purpose is not taught in school, it's not taught in your leadership training, it's not taught in sales training. I discovered it with the last living legend in the field of mindset, success and human potential. Discovering your purpose is a process. You don't decide on it. You don't create it. You develop yourself to the point where you live irrevocably committed to your purpose, then tap into your potential and then prosper – oh, do you ever prosper!

Suppose I can leave one lasting impression upon you. In that case, it is to forget everything you currently know and believe about yourself and to recreate yourself by discovering your purpose, untapping your potential and living a life of time and money freedom. If you are reading this and feel that "enough is enough" moment overcoming you, surrender and decide right here and now that this time it's going to be different for you too. This time you are going to listen to your inner coach and voice and begin the process of learning and discovering who you really are, why you're really here and what you really want. You have vast resources of talents and abilities, combined with infinite potential and you are here on purpose, with a purpose.

Don't you think it's time to step into your power, to step into your greatness and start creating the life you love to live?

Your purpose in this lifetime is to do the thing that you love. Your purpose gives meaning to why you are doing what you're doing. Vision is what you do with your life; it's the strategy behind the fulfillment of your purpose.

Vision is the key connector between one's potential and one's life purpose. Prosperity is doing what you want, when you want and with who you want. Prosperity is becoming more and more of who you are each day and enjoying a life of total freedom.

Who are you? Why are you here? What do you REALLY want? Discover and surrender to your purpose, untap your true infinite potential and prosper!

Meet Crystal McRae

From small town and scarcity to success and prosperity, Crystal McRae discovered her purpose and infinite potential. She now helps others realize their potential and dreams. How she adapted to this higher form of success is a very motivating and inspiring story. Through serious study and application of alternative education and personal development from teachers like Bob Proctor, Crystal turned her own personal experience into a duplicatable system to help people reach their true potential in health, wealth and happiness.

She is a Certified Consultant with Proctor Gallagher Institute, Member of Bob Proctor's Inner Circle, Founder of the Unblock Academy, motivational speaker, published author, success and results coach, and helps entrepreneurs and businesses achieve quantum leaps in their results, sales and success.

Website: www.unblockacademy.com
Email: crystal@unblockacademy.com

CHAPTER 4
"Stand Up and Shine… It's Your Time!"
By Noelle Ottenbreit

"Stand Up and Shine ... It's Your Time!"

- Noelle Ottenbreit

Calling the girl in the back of the room.

Yeah you! Hello there beautiful soul! What are you waiting for? Are you really shining? Or are you sitting in the shade, letting everyone around you shine? Seriously, take a deep breath right now. Take a deep breath, stand up proud of the body you are in, walk straight up to the front of the room and get on that stage. It's your time to shine! Shine? What do I mean by shine? I mean, step into the true you and the life that you genuinely want to live!

Ok, let's get serious. Do you believe in the words in this next sentence? Everything you think about can truly be yours! I know, I know, that sounds crazy. You want a million dollars and that hasn't happened yet. YET! That's the keyword.

Have you sat and thought about all the ways you would truly utilize one million dollars? How would you spend your days? What would you buy? How would you live? I am guessing probably not. Most of us haven't.

We like the *idea* of one million dollars! We've seen others with lots of money and have thought, "Wow, how well do they have it! Must be nice."

You can have it too! There is a secret to getting what you truly want in all areas of your life, and no, it's not working harder! It's a healthy obsession with not living without what you truly desire.

What is your true desire?

That question shook me too. I had no idea; I had thoughts, but I thought about it and then I carried on, probably laughing at myself at the moment too. Until that one bright sunshining morning when I got up and my family was still sleeping. I walked out to the kitchen, poured myself a coffee, sat down, opened up my bank app and thought, "Well, that's not enough to do all the things I need to do today, tomorrow or the next 14 days until the next same amount of money rolls into this account!".

I'd had it! I felt defeated and I was stuck in the habit of spinning more plates than I could handle for the same amount of money and never getting ahead. Just barely making it paycheck to paycheck. I know I am not the only one that's been there but I am here to tell you, you do not need to stay there. That's when the magic, or should I say my breaking point, happened and kicked me into manifestation.

I was instantly in la-la-land about getting a better outcome for all my hard work and effort. I was always making sure everyone was happy and taken care of and I forgot about myself! I made the decision, I needed to be happy and successful. I knew something had to give, I needed something more and I needed help! I screamed to the universe to show me a sign and just help me change my reality. It was my time to shine!

I didn't know where to start as I stared out the window, past the lane, across the bright wheat field as far as my eyes could see to the horizon. I pleaded with myself that it was time to be happy and find myself. That day was day one, I decided. I started to study the best material on the planet, *"Thinking Into Results,"* and my life hasn't been the same since. I had to get uncomfortable being comfortable or I knew nothing was going to change. I learned how to use my mind and imagination and how to manifest anything I truly want.

I have learned who I am and what my purpose is here on this wonderful planet. But most of all, I have learned that we all can do this! We can all have anything we want – if you can think it, you can hold it in your hand! Is it simple? Hell no! Do I have days or weeks where I fall off track and wonder what the hell is going on? Hell yeah! However, I do not unpack there.

I rise above and get real with myself, which isn't always the easiest, but it's the most necessary step in living on purpose, in my purpose. I have felt selfish for wanting more, I have worried about what other people will think or say, I have doubted myself, fought the inner warrior telling me to "play it safe," "sit back down," and "who do you think you are?" But in the end, not one of those feelings or questions are relevant. What was relevant was what was right for my family and me. What do I want that will help me succeed? That's the step forward. That was a must I had to make.

The manifestation and the little nudge from inside my soul is the spark that will light my way, day in and day out. It was up to me to make my dreams my reality and it is up to you to do the same.

You've got this, I promise.

Do not sit at the back of the room any longer. Let your voice be heard. Show your talents, dance in the rain, do every single little thing that starts you in the right direction to your soul's purpose of happiness. Be so proud of your soul, your body, and smile, always smile. Manifest with your whole heart, because you deserve everything you've ever wanted! In fact, you deserve more! You are you! You are deserving, and you get to make all your dreams come true!

Never stop dreaming.

It's your time to shine!

Meet Noelle Ottenbreit

Noelle Ottenbreit was born and raised in Saskatchewan where she lives with her husband, Jared and their three daughters, Jayana, Brexlyn and Aamyra. Noelle is an entrepreneur who spends her days living to the fullest, fulfilling her dreams of helping others seek their potential and live in their true purpose. There is nothing more fulfilling to Noelle than helping others and putting a smile on their faces. Noelle retired from her corporate Property Management position at 37 to chase her dreams of time and money freedom, continue her self development studies and simply live life to the fullest. Noelle is truly honoured to be a Co-Author in this E-book, as writing in a book was one of her 2021 bucket list items.

CHAPTER 5
"New Beginnings"
By Sherry Richter

"If you must doubt something, doubt your limits."

- Bob Proctor

Have you ever felt lost and alone?

Even though you're surrounded by a lot of people, people who love you and you love them?

That was me, every day. I had lost myself. I had retired from a long healthcare career and was wondering what's next. What am I going to do? I was okay for a while and then I started to feel useless, hopeless, with no purpose. Nothing.

I was feeling alone. I was worried about how I would live on my income, how I would keep my network marketing company going and how I was going to do anything. I felt responsible and I felt a duty to make things better.

I felt like I was drowning and I had no idea what to do. Who was I? Who am I? I mean, really, who am I? I felt like I lost my identity and I felt worthless.

I needed to make a change. I felt I had no label; Oh, I work for "blah blah blah," I'm so and so, and I do *this*. Well, I was doing nothing. Do we need a label? I felt like a failure! Like an imposter! I didn't feel worthy about a damn thing. I felt like I was carrying a burden I didn't want to bear. And I wasn't sure why; it's just how I felt.

I knew there had to be something better, but I didn't know how to get there or how to change or what to even do about it all. A friend suggested that I make an appointment with Crystal. She might have something that you'd be interested in.

I booked an appointment with her to go for coffee. What did I do? I sat and I cried and I bawled and I didn't know why. Crystal was like my angel in disguise, she told me there was a better way to think and do things and I would truly need a telescope to see how far I've gone in six months! I trusted her guidance and I knew things would be different.

I started working on the program and trusted in the process, and knew this would be different. Even though I didn't understand it all, I was excited. However, I was still terrified that things wouldn't change but somehow I just *knew* that I would learn and grow and discover new things along the way.

I can't even explain how I felt that day, I felt like there was hope for me to be ME and broaden my horizons!

I started doing the lessons in Thinking Into Results. This was something I had never done before. I had always been a positive person but this was so different. As I peeled the layers off my thoughts and ideas, what I thought was right and true, wasn't so much. I didn't realize that so many things had affected me in so many ways. I had these things called paradigms, so many of them and their habitual ways of doing things and beliefs. I could feel hope rising. I could feel my purpose coming alive. I could feel like new beginnings were coming.

I started to think differently, feel differently and realised that I was the only person that could change things. I began to react to things differently, too. In fact, I started responding and not reacting! I realised that my thoughts started to become things and that I had all the power I ever needed inside me to do and be anything I wanted to be!

I felt hope, felt empowered and felt like it was time to be who I was meant to be. I was the only ME there is on the planet. Do you realize that? There is ONLY ONE YOU!

Be who you were meant to be. You are perfectly perfect. You are God's perfect image of you and you have all the power inside you to do and be anything you want to be.

I started to attract things and I started to see things so differently. You know when someone says, "There's hardly any white vehicles on the road," guess what you begin to see? WHITE!

I started to see prosperity and purpose in my life and it kept happening. You start to see so much, things start to show up and you cannot explain it except *you attracted it*!

I have changed my mindset and not only have I started to empower others, but I truly have manifested so much in my life.

The power of attraction, the power of manifestation - we have it all within us. I had it the entire time and only needed to tap into it and believe I could do anything I put my mind to. Mindset is so important and I learned that anything is possible through the program called Thinking Into Results.

I thought I knew how to set a goal but I didn't even know what a goal was. I certainly do now! I set them and achieve them every day, week and month!

I truly understand how gratitude and love can change your life. Being grateful and appreciative for everything, how prosperity comes alive when you see things differently.

Go out and grab the world, it's all yours!

Meet Sherry Richter

Sherry Richter is a wife, mother and grandmother and has the most amazing family. She's a published author in the #1 best seller anthology, *Broken Trust*; an entrepreneur in her NWM Health and Wellness Arbonne company, has an up and coming business called Flourish and Believe Academy to promote confidence and empowerment in women of all ages.

Sherry is a member of The Unblock Academy, Thinking Into Results program as well as Lead the Field. Sherry continues to grow and thrive in this ever changing world and knows the best is yet to come.

CHAPTER 6
"Purpose Driven Pashion"
By Roxanne Pashniak

"Find your passion and follow your heart. This is how you will live in your purpose, potential and prosperity."

- Roxanne Pashniak

I remember sitting in my car.

The feelings of worry and fear were so overwhelming. I remember thinking, how did I get here? When will things start to get better? Three years and the struggle continued; I had been working so hard every day, trying harder to move forward from this mess I'm in! I prayed for help and I asked for a sign.

At that moment, I had no idea that everything was about to shift. I reached out for help. I didn't know how but one thing I knew for sure was that my way was not working. I decided that day. No savings in the bank and no means to invest in myself. All I knew was I never wanted to be in this place again ever, and I committed to doing whatever it took. Within two weeks, I had enrolled in The Diamond Success Mentorship Program with The Unblock Academy.

I recall the moment I realized that I had become a slave to the grind and my business for the past ten years, and what I wanted was freedom, but what I really felt was trapped! I had convinced myself that what I was doing would give us time and money freedom one day, but I was stuck on the hamster wheel! I worked to save costs and increase profitability. However, it seemed I would make some small gains, then I would fall back and I was frustrated.

I didn't know what I didn't know, I did not realize there was a better way. I did not know how my beliefs and feelings about myself, sales, money and the economy along with my circumstance, were responsible for the results I was getting.

When I became aware that it was completely in my ability to change, I didn't want to waste any more time trying harder trying to figure this out on my own. I was working so hard but getting more of the same results. I was stuck in a mindset of lack; I had only just scratched the surface of what was truly possible and what my purpose was! What I realized was that the more I worked on my mindset, the more freedom I experienced. I discovered that the freedom I was seeking was not outside of me - the key to freedom was in my mind!

The more I studied and applied what I was learning, the more I came to realize that I had a bigger purpose and a desire to serve and make a bigger impact! As I started to build the vision of my worthy ideal, Inspiring Pashion was created and my purpose and passion for helping others begin their Path to Freedom. The more I shifted, the more I could not ignore this calling. I didn't want to waste any more of my life settling for less than I was capable of achieving.

Steve Bow said, and I wholeheartedly agree, that *"God's gift to you is more talent and ability than you could possibly use in your lifetime, your gift to God is to develop as much of that talent and ability as you can in this lifetime."*

As I uncovered my purpose and potential, I began to transition from working full-time in my restaurant business to create space and time freedom to focus on my goals and exciting changes. The world shifted into the pandemic. Once again, I found myself controlled by circumstance but this time I was different and I had a community, a mentor and an idea. With the looming closure of businesses, I found myself with a lot of produce and product in my restaurant.

While on a mastermind session, I decided that while I had no control of restrictions, mandates, or closures, I could control what I would do. Rather than risk a lot of food going to waste, I decided to give. We prepared platters of food and delivered the food to some frontline workers in our local hospital, emergency services and other health care providers. I took to social media to see if our customers and community wanted to help. All the food that first day was sponsored by the amazing people who loved the idea.

Due to the fantastic support, I thought, *how can we stop there?* There were so many other frontline workers that I wanted to reach. Over the next few weeks, I reached out to see who we could serve and I spoke to others who wanted to be a part of the Sponsor a Lunch initiative. We were doing doorstep deliveries for families who were in isolation as they returned from travel. We were delivering food to the Health Unit and the grocery store frontline workers. I found a way to bring hope to social media and the community through one idea that God gave me.

The *"Sponsor A Lunch"* Program within the franchise formed, and the idea reached communities across Canada. It was a beautiful thing. Everything originates from thought and it sends out ripple effects further than I will probably ever know. I felt a strong sense of purpose and passion for helping more people experience this.

I know without a doubt that our business was blessed through a very challenging time, and the ripple effect carried forward into August when we hosted a customer appreciation day. We had one of our highest sales days on a Wednesday, during Covid. I had an overwhelming feeling of gratitude and prosperity! If I had any doubt left within me that we can create our economy, it was gone.

The economy in Alberta had not improved. During Covid, it had gotten worse, and we were able to see an increase we had not seen in a few years. The more I changed what was going on within me, the more everything in my life was improving.

Through my journey with Unblock Academy, the development of my mind and higher mental faculties, I transformed my self-image, realized my purpose and tapped into my infinite potential, prosperity and profit. I found so much fulfillment through creating Inspiring Pashion and discovering how to make a greater impact. Now, I love to help others discover their Path to Freedom and the Diamond Success Mentorship Program!

Meet Roxanne Pashniak

Roxanne Pashniak is an Empowerment Coach and Transformational Speaker. She founded Inspiring Pashion Empowerment Coaching and Self Image Consulting to help others transform from the inside out. As she uncovered a deeper purpose, Inspiring Pashion came to life to Ignite Passion, Inspire Action and Impact the World in a positive and profound way. She resides in Ardmore, Alberta Canada with her beautiful family. Roxanne enjoys writing and is a best-selling Co-Author of *Broken Trust*.

Roxanne studied Human Potential and the Mind at the Proctor Gallagher Institute in affiliation with The Unblock Academy. As a Diamond Executive Success Advisor with The Unblock Academy, she guides others to their path to freedom by empowering them to bring their gifts, talents and infinite potential to the surface. Then they can step into their higher calling and self image and discover their purpose, potential and prosperity.

CHAPTER 7
"Awareness and Growing into Prosperity"
By Jocelyne St-Jacques

"The key to a
prosperous life
was discovering
who I am."

- Jocelyne
St-Jacques

I do not know about you, but I have talked to many people who have said that the year 2020 was not a great year.

For me, being laid off because of certain circumstances that happened that year was probably the best thing that had ever happened to me. I had never been laid off from a job before, so this was my first time and my last time. At first, I did not know what to do with myself because, at that time, I thought going to work was *the* way of life.

I never really enjoyed my jobs, even though I went through school to get where I was and was making money to pay my bills. I was not yet aware that life did not have to be that way - that I could spend my days doing what I want, when I want, with whomever I want. I always felt like I had a higher purpose and was worth more than what I was putting myself through in life.

At that time, I was also working at healing my body naturally from an autoimmune disease. While on my healing journey of mainly changing my diet, a close friend introduced to me the healing powers of meditation. I then came across other self-help practices such as journaling, listening to podcasts and reading a great number of books. Some worked for a little bit but the results never stuck.

I continued searching for a better, healthier, more fulfilling life and I could not seem to find something that provided permanent results. It got to the point where I wanted a change, and I was tired of my results and how my life was going. I did, however, have a strong feeling everything was about to get better.

Before I knew it, I found the solution: The Unblock Academy. The Unblock Academy isn't just some group. It is a community filled with like-minded people who want to improve their lives drastically, learn more about themselves and achieve permanent, quick and effective results. I was in this group for half a year, but it was not until it finally came into my awareness that I truly was a part of this community. I remember saying that the positivity that came from this community was unreal - it was and still is so powerful. I also felt that I had never really been around so much support for a better life, especially from so many people I did not know.

Just being a part of this community almost immediately helped me discover what I wanted to do with my life: own and live on an acreage with a U-pick berry farm and store where I sell handmade, homemade and homegrown products created by others and myself. This goal would also be my opportunity to show many people how to live consciously and sustainably. What better way to help the environment, apply the schooling I had received in Environmental Engineering Technology and inspire and help others get through their healing journey than to start a berry farm and handmade store?

Very soon after, I was presented with the opportunity to enroll in an amazing personal development program called Thinking into Results, where I began to study how powerful my mind is. I do not even consider it a program; it is more like learning a new lifestyle, a lifelong commitment always to be creating and growing.

Having a big goal that excites me yet makes me sick was the first step to living a meaningful life. The vibration that I am on when thinking, feeling, writing, and talking about my U-pick goal is unbelievable.

With my passion and love for helping the environment and all living beings on this planet, along with my desire for a healthy and happy life, I suddenly realised that this was my purpose; helping others and the environment live a long, happy and healthy life too.

Like every other human being on this planet, I realised that I have infinite potential and can, be, do and have anything I want. This allowed me to retire from working at a corporate 9-5 job at the age of twenty-seven. This was a huge decision that I never thought I would make in my lifetime, especially during a pandemic but I learned that I could never let circumstances dictate how I live my life. I now live in time freedom, where I decide what I want to do, whenever I want to do it. I never thought this was even a possibility but it's one of the best feelings in the world.

Becoming aware that I have infinite potential has changed my perception of life, and all I wanted to do since that realization was to share this valuable information with others. Currently, I am a Success Advisor for the Unblock Academy. Being a part of this team has allowed me to share with others what has changed my life to have a more fulfilling and happy life as well.

I became the founder of a natural, handmade products business called Dandee-Care Natural Products. I found and developed a way of helping others and the environment by making safe-to-use products using one of the most beneficial and persistent flowers found right in my backyard, the dandelion. I never imagined even starting my own business, let alone a successful business that has provided amazing results to many people.

It is amazing what a simple decision to invest in myself did to allow my awareness to expand and grow every day. For me, the key to a prosperous life was discovering who I am. I am forever thankful for the Unblock Academy community, Thinking into Results and all those who have supported me to be me.

Meet Jocelyne St-Jacques

Jocelyne St-Jacques recently moved to Buchanan, SK with her boyfriend of 13 years and their dog named Bandit. She graduated with great distinction in both Dental Assisting as well as Environmental Engineering Technology. One of Jocelyne's greatest passions is teaching others how to live consciously and sustainably-doing anything she can to help the planet and others' well-being.

Jocelyne's personal health journey led her to become the founder of a natural, handmade products company called Dandee-Care Natural Products, where she creates a variety of products using dandelions. Her love to help others shines through her work as a Success Advisor for the Unblock Academy. Jocelyne wants everyone to become aware of his or her infinite potential, just as she has, and to take action.

CHAPTER 8
"You Show More, You Flow Higher"
By Shreesha Khare

Inside the womb of the divine feminine,
purpose, potential and prosperity were our
birthrights. But outside the womb, we created a
scripture to follow purpose, potential, and
prosperities like it is a herculean task.

After trying, failing, and hitting rock bottom
every single time, I awakened to enlightenment.
I entered the womb of darkness as an adult, just
to see how I am designed to hold blessings, just
like a water bottle is designed to hold water.

Potential is an invisible, unbroken umbilical cord
that connects us to our Purpose. We are bonded
with our Purpose. No matter what vicious cycle
we find ourselves in, our true calling will always
call us home.

Prosperity is natural. It comes with Purpose and
Potential in terms of growth, richness, and
learning. Just like fruits on a tree know their
duties, there is no fight. There is no struggle.
Their purpose is to give, and potential helps us
stay strong no matter what we face in the
seasons of our lives.

- Shreesha Khare

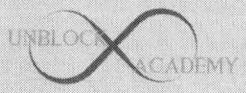

A piece of wood went to a sculptor and asked him to make her beautiful.

The sculptor said, "Sure, I can do that. Are you ready for it?"

The wood said, "Yes, indeed, I am ready." The sculptor started the grinding process for wood. It started feeling fearful and painful, the wood said that it was good to go for today, but the sculptor focused on making the wood beautiful. The day ended and the wood was ready as a great deity or house; it received appreciation and applause.

The purpose of wood is to burn, to go through hard machinery objects to convert into pleasing home décor. Wood knows its purpose. It is always on fire to bring out the best of its capabilities in itself, and when wood burns, people pay the price to keep it. We can think of a thing's purpose as its nature; the nature of a tea kettle is to have tea in it. The nature of the saw is to cut and so on. It is easy to identify the purpose of a tea kettle and saws are pretty simple, but can the same logic be applied to a more complex creation; humans?

Rock bottom comes into our lives as if someone barged into the room quickly without knocking, which is exactly what happened to me on Oct. 7th, 2019. My life was crumbling down piece by piece. I vividly remember how I was frustrated and fired up about my corporate job for three years as Human Resource Analytics for a London-based organisation, where I started my career and ended it forever. It gave me a realization that my life is just more than sitting behind the laptop and doing crazy transactions and project handling.

Sitting in my office cabin, I was praying to God and Angels to help me move out of this situation full of manipulation as the work I was doing was not bringing out the best of me. It was not making me do what I love, to make a difference in people. I already set the tone for writing that I used to express my thoughts and experiences with others day in and day out. I used that experience to write my first book in January 2019, *Along the Way*. I wrote about self-love and relationships, where I shared some of my experiences from my London days.

I wrote that book when I was working, but the thought was, *"It is just a hobby."* I took the risk and challenged myself to be a risk-taker. Putting myself in an uncomfortable zone comes naturally to me but I was not ready to accept this fact.

I was okay with my comfort zone because I was getting a paycheck in my bank every month, but deep down, I was stuck. I created this illusionary wall that never existed where I was thinking,

"I am stuck. I can't move. Someone is stopping me from doing what I want to do." But the question was, what *did* I want to do?

Learning never stopped for me, I was always a person who worked on herself every single day since the time I gained consciousness, I never stopped learning. After my office hours, I used to study and learn. I enrolled myself in weekend classes which helped me to gain confidence. I believed that working on my Intellectual ability supported me to stand in front of a larger audience, which was the turning point in my life.

In 2020, I sacked myself out of the corporate world as Human Resource Analytics. I didn't know what I would do or how I would replace my monthly paycheck. I gained clarity on that; I am made for the leadership level and not for taking rules from someone else. I love being my own boss rather than allowing someone else to rule over me. Some people called me fanatical for the path I have chosen for myself, but we all need rock bottom to realize who we are and why we are here on this earth.

Learning helped me to answer these questions. We are designed in a certain way to serve the community. Understanding our purpose and the potential we hold takes more than just a day or two; it takes constant drilling into uncomfortable things, taking risks, and putting oneself in challenging situations. These experiences enlighten you to walk on your core path, which comes naturally only to you.

Purpose is Dharma, a Sanskrit word which means things come naturally to you. Your calling is combined with natural talents and passion (what we love to do) with the Universe's needs (working for a larger community), and that becomes our purpose.

The unprecedented times in my life brought changes that arrived like an explosion. It made me realize that my writings come naturally to me; being philosophical and guiding comes naturally to me. I love helping people with my skills, knowledge, talent and experience.

I am designed as an inspirational thought leader who holds a deep internal desire to take all of what I have learned and help others along the path. I feel called at my soul level to share my true self with the world. My life is all about personal mastery and optimal growth. I want to learn as much as I can and help other people to transform their lives. I advanced myself at a spiritual, mental, and physical level, which makes me get up in the morning.

My power lives in my resiliency, personal experiences, and ability to inspire and teach. I lead by example and show people what is possible when you choose love over fear. I am a Servant Leader, a luminary light who shines brighter, and this gave birth to Melon and Summon, a brand that works with the tagline, "Own Who You Are." My knowledge, high thinking ability and my writings on different platforms show how it makes a difference in people.

I am creating a business based on my skills and knowledge by being an Author and Speaker. I love knowing that I have the power to teach people and improve their lives. There are times when we look at these things in certain ways, like *"I must earn this much and have this lifestyle."* Still, when we serve our purpose and potential by bringing out our gifts and sharing with a larger audience, then prosperity automatically follows. When we earn people's respect, live a life of true credibility and service, prosperity is bound to arrive at our doorstep.

Meet Shreesha Khare

Shreesha Khare is India's Top Debut Author of *Along the Way*, a book about Self-Love and Relationships. She is also a Global Speaker, Podcaster, Spiritual Being, Explorer and Chief Human Designer for Humanity. She chose a career in Human Resource Management with a Master's Degree from Nottingham Trent University, London, England and worked for three years in the corporate world as a Human Resource Analyst. She believes that her degree is here to serve her and not vice-versa.

Learning never stops for her. There is nothing in the world she has not studied to develop her personality, from Mindvalley's Best Masterclass Teachers to Bob Proctor teachings. She is a proud member of Unblock Academy and Proctor Gallagher Institute and part of the program "Thinking Into Results."

Her purpose is to share her personal narratives which set the tone for her life experiences and the direction her life takes. She believes that this isn't about her own life. She believes that we all live a story within a bigger story: a story of humanity on planet earth.

CHAPTER 9
"You Always Have a Cheerleader in Your Back Pocket"
By Jessica Jones

"There is only one you. That is your power. Allow yourself to shine like the star you are!"

- Jessica Jones

You are amazing!

Yes, YOU! Probably not something that you remind yourself every day but you definitely should. Heck, start today! Remember, you need to be your biggest cheerleader first and foremost. It's time you put yourself first. Get ready to love yourself: all the parts, the good and the bad. I know what you're thinking, easier said than done. Trust me, just keep reminding yourself:

DO NOT GIVE UP, YOU ARE WORTH IT!

I'll admit, this is not something that came to me quickly, which is why I'm sharing this with you. I don't want you to take your whole life to come to this realization. I've been the cheerleader for so many people and watched their dreams come true for years. Let me start by saying, I don't regret that at all. I love supporting my family and friends, I always will. However, somewhere along the way, I forgot about myself. Somewhere, I forgot that my dreams counted too. Why is it we always put ourselves last? That is the one thing most of us have in common.

For me, I had my "enough is enough" moment. It was time to get back on track. I wanted more for myself and especially for my family. I didn't want to continue to be stuck. I didn't want to continue to live paycheck to paycheck. I didn't want to just go through the motions as I currently was. I'm sure you can relate. I have not taken many risks. For most of my life, I have played it safe and nothing was changing. It was something I observed from a lot of people in my life.

I can still hear them saying,

"Yeah, but is it safe?"

"Is it stable and secure?"

In their defense, most people we know spend their whole lives playing it safe. I don't blame them for what they didn't know. It's important to know you cannot change what you do not know. It's a continuous cycle and you need to choose to stop it.

Some people in my life took risks but they weren't considered "normal." Those were the people that were watched closely, judged and everyone secretly wanted them to fail. They would never admit it but it's true.

Secretly, I was envious of them. They just went for it. They didn't know how. They didn't figure out the details. They just had the desire and nothing was going to stop them from getting their goal. If they weren't successful, they would regroup, figure out a different way or make the necessary adjustment to ensure they won. So here I was, it came to the point where I had to decide to live, like really live the life I deserve. It was time to live up to my true life *potential*.

Finally, I was ready. I decided to study the best material on the planet, "Thinking Into Results," with the support of the Unblock Academy. Once I made a decision, everything fell into place. I knew my life would change, there was no going back, it was time for me to shine!

The first step was to focus on me. I needed to work on the inside of me and unleash my *purpose*. I needed to put as much energy into myself as I was with everyone else. I was putting myself first. I knew that I needed to ensure I was strong on the inside and that my paradigms weren't getting in the way or stopping me from reaching my goals. I was ready to step into living on purpose, in my purpose.

I am not going to pretend working on the inside stuff isn't easy, there were lots of uncomfortable days and moments. Some days were better than others. Roadblocks appeared, some huge ones, and some days I thought about throwing up my hands and stopping but I didn't. I kept showing up for myself each day and showing up to become better than the day before. It would have been easy to quit, it's what I have always done. I had to trust. Trust in the material and trust in me. Trust that I was worth it.

That's why I'm writing this, to remind you that you are worth it! Yes, you are. Leap! Bet on yourself. Choose you every time. You see, you can have anything you want. If you can imagine it, you can make it happen, as long as it does not cause harm to anyone else. You can make it your reality. You have to truly desire it. It needs to motivate you like nothing else.

I've been challenged and faced huge decisions throughout my journey. The key was I didn't give up. Since putting me first, so much good has happened for my family and me. I wake up every day so grateful for all the opportunities that I've been blessed with. I know that this is just the beginning of greater things to come.

I encourage everybody to invest in themselves and take the first step.

YOU ARE WORTH IT!

Don't let fear stop you in your tracks and be brave enough to break through the chains that are holding you back. If you feel doubt creeping in at any time, know you always have this chapter in your back pocket. I am cheering you on and wish you all the best and all your dreams to come true.

YOU'VE GOT THIS!

Meet Jessica Jones

Jessica Jones was born and raised in Saskatchewan. She now lives in Manitoba with her partner of 10 years, Cliff. Jessica is a proud bonus mom to three; Zhané, Caeden and Marcus. She is grateful to be a mama to her granddaughter Violet. Writing a book was one of Jessica's goals for 2021 and she feels truly blessed to be a Co-Author in this E-book.

Jessica has been with her corporate career for eleven years. Her career has allowed her to strengthen her leadership roles. This has helped Jessica and her staff achieve their goals and exceed in their roles. Jessica enjoys helping others seek their potential and live in their purpose.

THE BEGINNING

Elite Services We Offer:

Real Help. Real Results. Real Fast.

GOAL SETTING AND ACHIEVING

Using a proven, scientific process we can identify blind spots
and help you achieve your goals.

TIME & MONEY FREEDOM

We provide tools to build wealth creation, debt elimination
and multiple sources of income.

HIGH PERFORMANCE

We offer consulting and business development for
corporations, small businesses, entrepreneurs, sales teams.

DISCOVER WORK LIFE BALANCE

We teach you how to multiply your effectiveness without
trying harder and doing more.

IF YOU'RE READING THIS, IT'S TIME.

It's time to transform your *dreams* into **REALITY,** your *goals* into **ACHIEVEMENTS** and your *thoughts* into **RESULTS.**

This one-of-a-kind Success System is based on nearly 60 years of intensive research into the science and mechanics of Personal Achievement, exploring what makes successful people successful.

Developed by world-renowned success expert Bob Proctor and legendary corporate attorney Sandy Gallagher, it is the most powerful process ever created for quickly and permanently transforming your goal, dream, or desire into reality.

The Unblock Academy Success System & Mentorship Program is designed to facilitate positive profound permanent change in any area of your life including debt elimination, multiple sources of income, wealth creation, a new home, improved health or ANY GOAL YOU CHOOSE.

What makes our Success System so extraordinarily effective?

- **In depth, individual lessons** focus intensively on a single essential element of the achievement process, with each lesson building upon the insights of the last. In fact, **you will experience a Quantum Leap in your results from the first moment you begin this program.**

94

- **Worksheets and activities** challenge you to apply what you learn immediately, so you see and feel yourself changing, progressing, and moving closer to your goals in real-time. Through this targeted repetition, you will **quickly and automatically form the habits that lead to long-term prosperity and abundance.**
- **Dynamic videos** expand your awareness, empower you with the knowledge you need, motivate you, and reinforce the lesson content at multiple levels of consciousness - a critical key to achieving change.

You will permanently possess the power to get anything you truly want, in any area of your life, for the rest of your life.

Request a FREE Strategy Call today.

Email: clientcare@unblockacademy.com or visit us at www.unblockacademy.com

If you want something more out of life but aren't sure what it is... If you've tried to make changes in the past, without success... If you have a specific goal but don't know how to achieve it...

Here is some incredible news:

You can get anything you seriously want. Guaranteed.

Be more. Do more. Have more.

Starting today.

Manufactured by Amazon.ca
Bolton, ON